ApocalyptiGirl

ApocalyptiGirl™

An Aria for the End Times

by Andrew MacLean

®
Dark Horse Books

PRESIDENT AND PUBLISHER
MIKE RICHARDSON

EDITOR
JIM GIBBONS

DIGITAL PRODUCTION
CHRISTINA McKENZIE

COLLECTION DESIGN
TINA ALESSI

SPECIAL THANKS TO
JOHN ARCUDI AND MICHAEL AVON OEMING

PUBLISHED BY DARK HORSE BOOKS
A DIVISION OF DARK HORSE COMICS, INC.
10956 SE MAIN STREET
MILWAUKIE, OR 97222

FIRST EDITION: MAY 2015
ISBN 978-1-61655-566-5

1 3 5 7 9 10 8 6 4 2
PRINTED IN CHINA

INTERNATIONAL LICENSING: (503) 905-2377
COMIC SHOP LOCATOR SERVICE: (888) 266-4226

APOCALYPTIGIRL: AN ARIA FOR THE END TIMES

FROM THE GREEK AND LATIN "AER," MEANING ATMOSPHERE...
...THE WORD "ARIA" FIRST SHOWS UP IN RELATION TO MUSIC SOMETIME IN THE FOURTEENTH CENTURY.
EVENTUALLY THE TERM COMES TO MEAN "MUSIC WRITTEN FOR A SINGLE VOICE," USUALLY IN REGARDS TO OPERA.
IT'S ALSO MY NAME...

...AND IT'S BEAUTIFUL.
AH! JE RIS DE ME VOIR SI BELLE EN CE MIROIR, AH! JE RIS DE ME VOIR SI BELLE EN CE MIROIR, EST-CE TOI, MARGUERITE, EST-CE TOI?

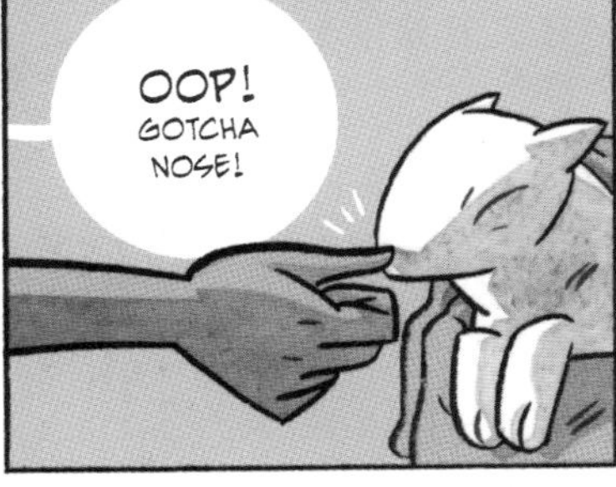

* "AH, JE RIS DE ME VOIR," MARGUERITE'S ARIA FROM THE OPERA **FAUST** BY CHARLES GOUNOD, 1859

WHAT?
YOU DON'T WANT YOUR NOSE?
I WAS GONNA GIVE IT BACK, YOU KNOW!

WELL, FINE!

DON'T MIND IF I DO.

HOMP!

lick lick

AND A HAPPY ANNIVERSARY TO YOU TOO, JELLY BEANS!

ALL RIGHT, GUS...
...LET'S SEE IF WE CAN'T GET YOU ON YOUR FEET TODAY.

PRETENDING A CAT IS YOUR BOYFRIEND?
KIND OF CREEPY-WEIRD.
LEAVE ME ALONE.
WELL...IT IS.

OH YEAH?! WELL, WHAT'S WITH ALL THAT "GREEK, LATIN, OPERA" CRAP?
WHAT, ARE YOU NARRATING YOUR OWN LIFE NOW?

tinktonk
GAH!
K-chok
SHE SAYS, RESPONDING TO THE VOICE IN HER HEAD.
klink

IT IS OUR ANNIVERSARY THOUGH...

I MET JELLY BEANS RIGHT HERE IN THIS COCKPIT...
...EXACTLY FIVE YEARS AGO TODAY.

ROOROOROO K-CHUNK

WHOA !

MOOCH

KOFF
KOFF KOFF
GAH! BUGGER.
cling cling BANG

HERE YOU ARE.

HEY, JELLY.
GUS POPPED ANOTHER CANISTER.
I KNOW! SUCH A GRUMP!

WELP! THIS SMOKE'LL BE VISIBLE FOR MILES...
...SO I'M THINKING IT'S ABOUT TIME WE POUND SAND, CHAMP.
READY?

OH! THANKS FOR GETTING DINNER, BY THE WAY!
A LITTLE SQUIRREL WILL GO GREAT WITH THE LAST OF THE APPLES!

. . .
I KNEW YOU REMEMBERED OUR ANNIVERSARY.

YOU KNOW, FOR AN APOCALYPSE...
...IT AIN'T ALL BAD.
YOU SEE THOSE PERFECT LITTLE LAKES CATCHING ALL THE COLOR?
THE BLUE STRIPES AND THE GREY BEARDS REFER TO THEM AS THE "TEARS OF THE SUN."
IN THEIR OWN GARBLED-UP LANGUAGES, OF COURSE.

A SEED WAS PLANTED IN THIS CITY. IT CAME WITH A PROMISE OF PEACE AND PROSPERITY, BUT YIELDED ONLY DEATH AND DESTRUCTION. THOSE WHO SOW A SEED TARNISHED AND ABUSED REAP A GARDEN OF EQUAL BEAUTY. NO ONE SURVIVED.

BUT ASH IS CARRIED AWAY ON THE WIND, AND WHAT IS TAKEN IS RECOVERED. NATURE RECLAIMS. EVEN AMONGST THE RUBBLE AND CRUMBLING TOWERS, THE CITY TEEMED WITH LIFE AGAIN. AND SO IN TIME, THE HUMANS RETURNED.

HERE THEY FOUND A FRESH START...

A NEW BEGINNING...

A FUTURE...

AND THEY DROWNED IT IN BLOOD.

THEIR LEGENDS SAY THAT A DAY CAME WHEN THE FIGHTING BETWEEN THE BLUE STRIPES AND THE GREY BEARDS (OR THAT'S WHAT I CALL THEM ANYWAY) INTENSIFIED UNTIL ALL THE WATER OF THE WORLD RAN RED WITH THE BLOOD OF THE SLAIN.

AND SO THE SUN, OF WHOM BOTH TRIBES REVERE, SAW HOW THE WATER HAD BEEN SPOILED, AND TOOK PITY ON HER PEOPLE.

BOTH TRIBES CLAIM TO BE "HER PEOPLE."

HER ***ONLY*** PEOPLE.

THE SUN SHED SOMBER TEARS OF FIRE ON THE CITY. STREAKING ACROSS THE SKY IN A THREE FINGERED ARC, THEY FELL AMONGST THE TREES AND EMPTY SHELLS OF BUILDINGS, PUSHING EVERYTHING BACK IN GREAT CLOUDS OF SWIRLING FLAME.

THE EXPLOSIONS LEFT THREE PERFECT CIRCLE CRATERS IN PERFECT TRIANGULAR FORMATION.

AS THE DUST SETTLED, THE MEN RETURNED TO THEIR WAR, AND THE EARTH RETURNED TO HEALING HER WOUNDS.
RAINWATER COLLECTED AND STREAMS THAT HAD BEEN DISRUPTED BY THE EXPLOSIONS ZIGZAGGED THROUGH THE RUBBLE TO FIND NEW PATHS. THE CRATERS FILLED WITH FRESH WATER, SWELLING INTO LAKES. PERFECT FOR BATHING. CLEAN ENOUGH TO DRINK.
A BLESSING FROM THE SUN TO "HER PEOPLE."
AND SO A WAR OF TERRITORY AND PETTY SQUABBLING TOOK ON A NEW FACE.
A FACE WRITTEN IN THE STARS. A FACE MENACING AND PRIDEFUL. NOT EVIL BY NATURE BUT EVIL BY DEED.
IT IS A WAR FOR HALLOWED GROUND THAT IS FOUGHT TODAY. FOR SACRED SOIL AND HOLY WATER.
THE WAR BETWEEN THE BLUE STRIPES AND THE GREY BEARDS...
...IS **HOLY**.

I'D LOVE TO GET GUS DOWN THERE TO DIG AROUND A BIT...
...BUT THEY'LL MAKE SUCH A STINK OF IT.
FLIK FLIK

PROW!

NOW, WHERE THE HELL IS HE--

ROFF
ROFF
ROFF
ROFF

ROFF ROFF
ROFF ROFF
ROFF
HUNTING DOGS.

BUGGER.
ROFF ROFF ROFF ROFF
ROFF

DAMN BLUE STRIPES HAVE BEEN COVERING MORE AND MORE TERRITORY LATELY.
ROFF ROFF ROFF ROFF
ROFF

ROFF ROFF ROFF ROFF ROFF
CAVED IN...
ALL THE EXITS...
BLOCKED...

ROFF ROFF
...EXCEPT ONE.

SMASH

BAMF

GET UP.
GET UP AND RUN.
UHHHHHH UHHH-UH!
CAN'T...
CAN'T BREATHE...

THERE!
NOW MOVE!
GASP

RRR.
GAH!

HHHHHH

HHHHHH

ROFF

THWIP

THUD!

JELLY...

...IT'S TIME TO GO.

...

PAK PAK
PAK PAK
CLOP CLOP

MIND THE BLADE, JELLY BEANS.

click

DOGS...
JUST DOGS...
SURVIVAL OF THE FITTEST...
KILL OR BE KILLED...

ALL THAT SHIT.

LET'S GET CLEANED UP, JELLY...
ONE

I FEEL DISGUSTING.

H
C

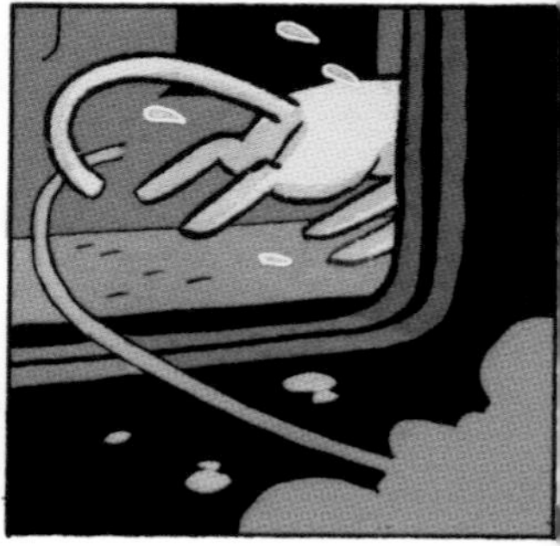

ALL RIGHT, LET'S SEE WHAT WE'VE GOT.

POOPED.
OUT.

G'NIGHT, JELLY BEANS.
HAPPY ANNIVERSARY.

click

BEEDLE DOOP DOOP

WHA?

BEEDLE DOOP DOOP

BEEDLE—
SHUT UP.
YESTERDAY WAS TOUGH...
...I'LL LET JELLY SIT THIS ONE OUT.

SIGNAL DETECTED
STRENGTH

GUS, THE OLD MECH IN THE PARK...

...HE HAD A JOB ONCE. A **MISSION**.

SAME AS MINE, IN FACT.

WHEN THE TRACKER FINDS A **SIGNAL**, WE FOLLOW IT. WE GO **SEARCHING**, LOOKING, NEVER MOVING ON UNTIL WE FIND THE SOURCE OF IT.

BUT GUS **FAILED** AND IS FORGOTTEN NOW, AND I FEAR I AM FORGOTTEN AS WELL.

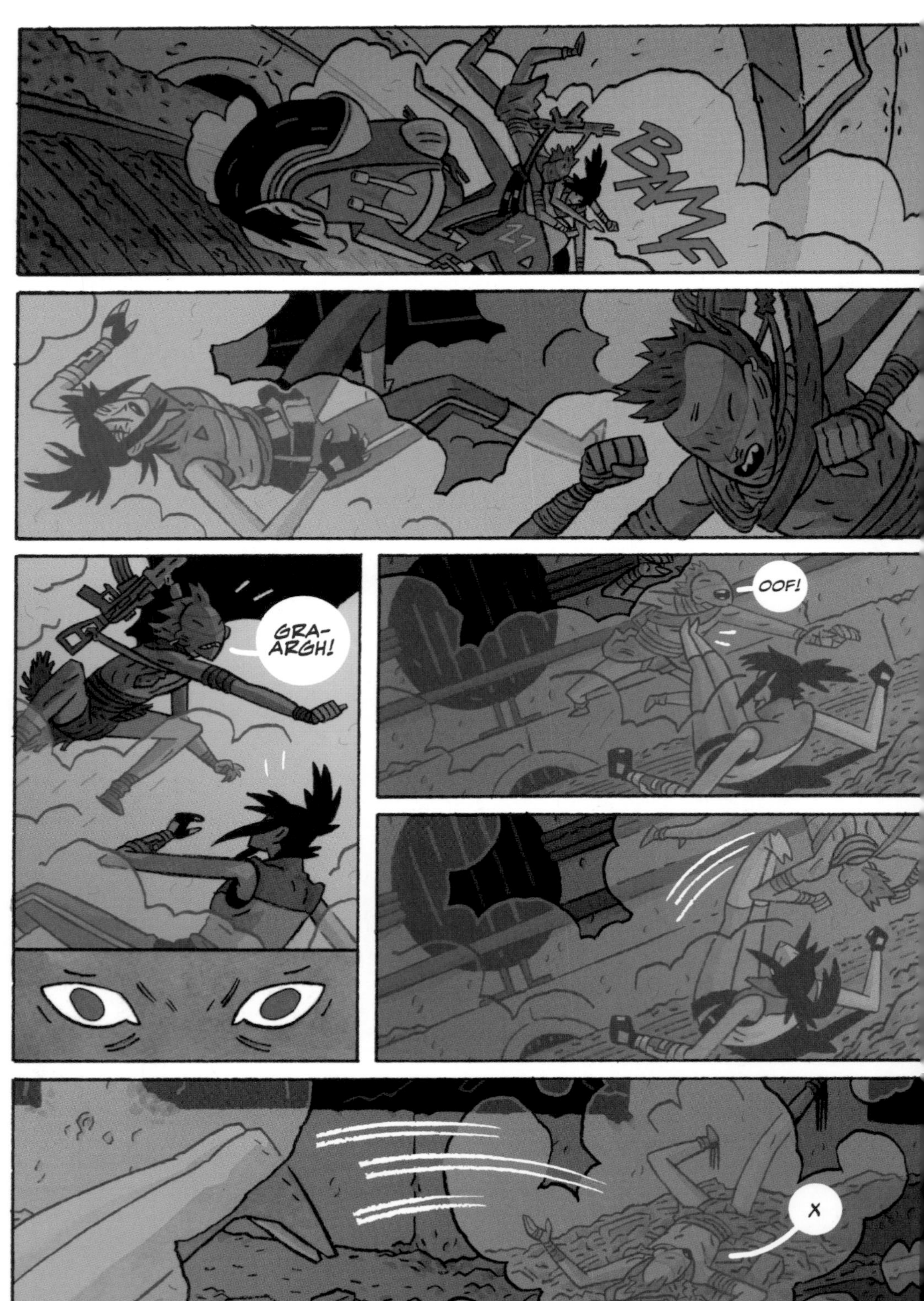
BAMF
GRA-
ARGH!
OOF!
X

VREEEEE

RUMBLE RUMBLE
HE MUST HAVE BEEN WANDERING THESE TUNNELS **ALL NIGHT**...

MY TUNNELS!
I SHOULD HAVE **KILLED** HIM!
RUMBLE RUMBLE

KILL HIM?! YOU REALLY TH--
SHIT! THE SIGNAL HAS **ALREADY** WEAKENED.

VREEEE

YES!
I SHOULD'VE KILLED THAT STUPID SHIT AND HIS DEAD STUPID SHIT EYES!
YOU'RE NO KILLER.

KILLED THOSE DOGS!
BESIDES, JELLY AND I HAVE BUILT A HOME DOWN THERE AND NOW THE KID KNOWS IT! IF HE TELLS HIS PEOPLE...
I SHOULD HAVE KILLED HIM...
...
...PROBABLY...
...BUT HE'S JUST A KID.

BEEE DOOP

LOST THE SIGNAL ...
AGAIN!

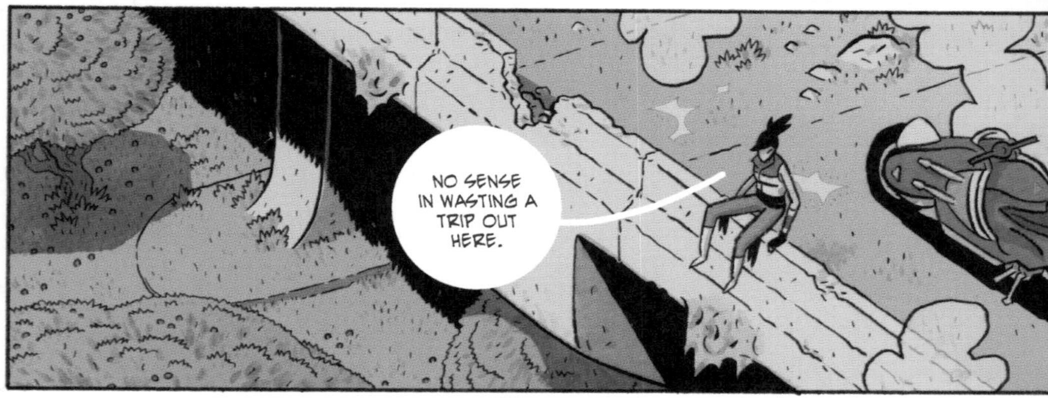
NO SENSE IN WASTING A TRIP OUT HERE.

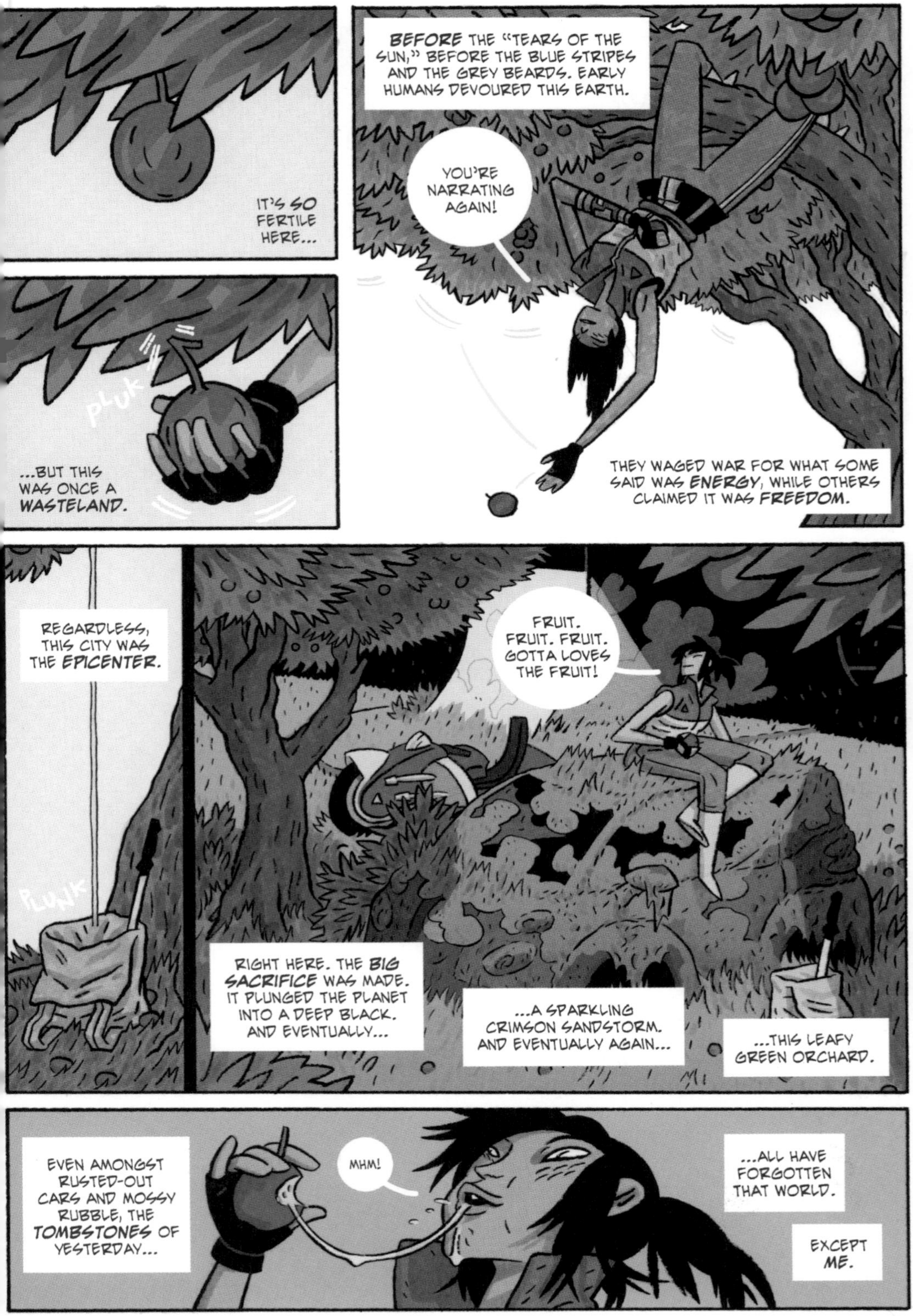

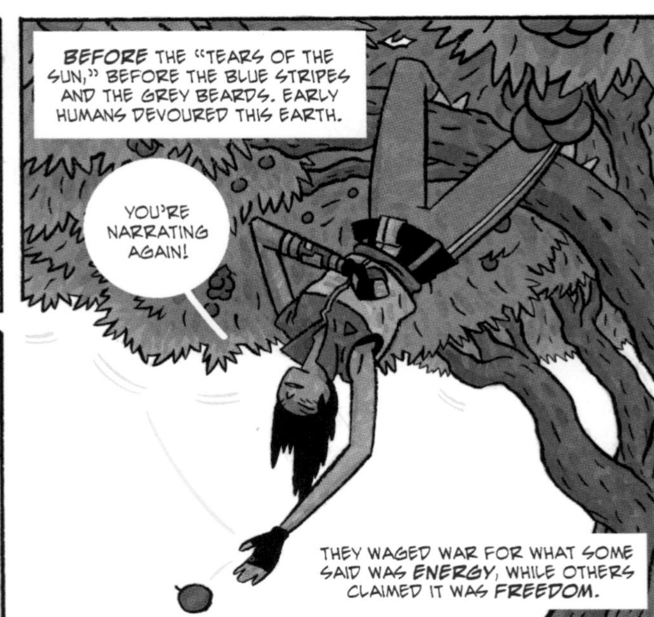

REGARDLESS, THIS CITY WAS THE EPICENTER.

PLUNK

FRUIT. FRUIT. FRUIT. GOTTA LOVES THE FRUIT!

RIGHT HERE. THE BIG SACRIFICE WAS MADE. IT PLUNGED THE PLANET INTO A DEEP BLACK. AND EVENTUALLY...

...A SPARKLING CRIMSON SANDSTORM. AND EVENTUALLY AGAIN...

...THIS LEAFY GREEN ORCHARD.

AH, BUGGER.

FINE, BONEHEADS! YOUR APPLES. I GET IT! I GET IT!
WHERE DO THEY EVEN GET GUNS?

NOPE.

THUD!

BRAKKA
BRAKKA
BRAKKA
BRAKKA
BRA
BRA
BRAK!

SPUK
SPUK
SPUK
SPUK
SPUK

PROW
PROW
PROW
PROW
VREE
SPUK
SPUK
PROW
REEE
K-CHIK
PROW
SPUK
SPUK

MY APPLES.

WAH! AH! AH!

JELLY BEEEANS !!!
I WENT HOME TO GET HIM BUT HE WASN'T THERE.

I SWEAR, IF THAT DEAD-EYED FREAK TOUCHED EVEN A HAIR...
JELLY ALMOST NEVER TAKES OFF ON HIS OWN.

JELLY BEANS?
BUT WHEN HE DOES...

HE ALWAYS ENDS UP IN THE SAME PLACE.

HSSSS

AH COOL IT, YA KNUCKLE-HEAD.

skritch skritch

*FROM "LASCIA CH'IO PIANGA," ALMIRENA'S ARIA FROM THE OPERA "RINALDO" BY GEORGE FRIDERIC HANDEL, 1711.

DURING THE AGE OF THE ONE, A SELF-SUSTAINING ENERGY SOURCE WAS DISCOVERED ON THE BOTTOM OF THE OCEAN.
A GRAND PHOTON.

IT WAS PERFECT ENERGY, A GIFT FROM ABOVE. IN THE RIGHT HANDS IT COULD TURN AN ENTIRE PLANET INTO A VERITABLE EDEN.
PARADISO.

BUT AS IT TURNED OUT, FATE WAS CRUEL TO THIS PLANET.
BOOM!

THE ONE HELD THE GRAND PHOTON HOSTAGE, DENYING ALL BUT THEIR OWN ITS PLENTIFUL GIFTS.
CHOK

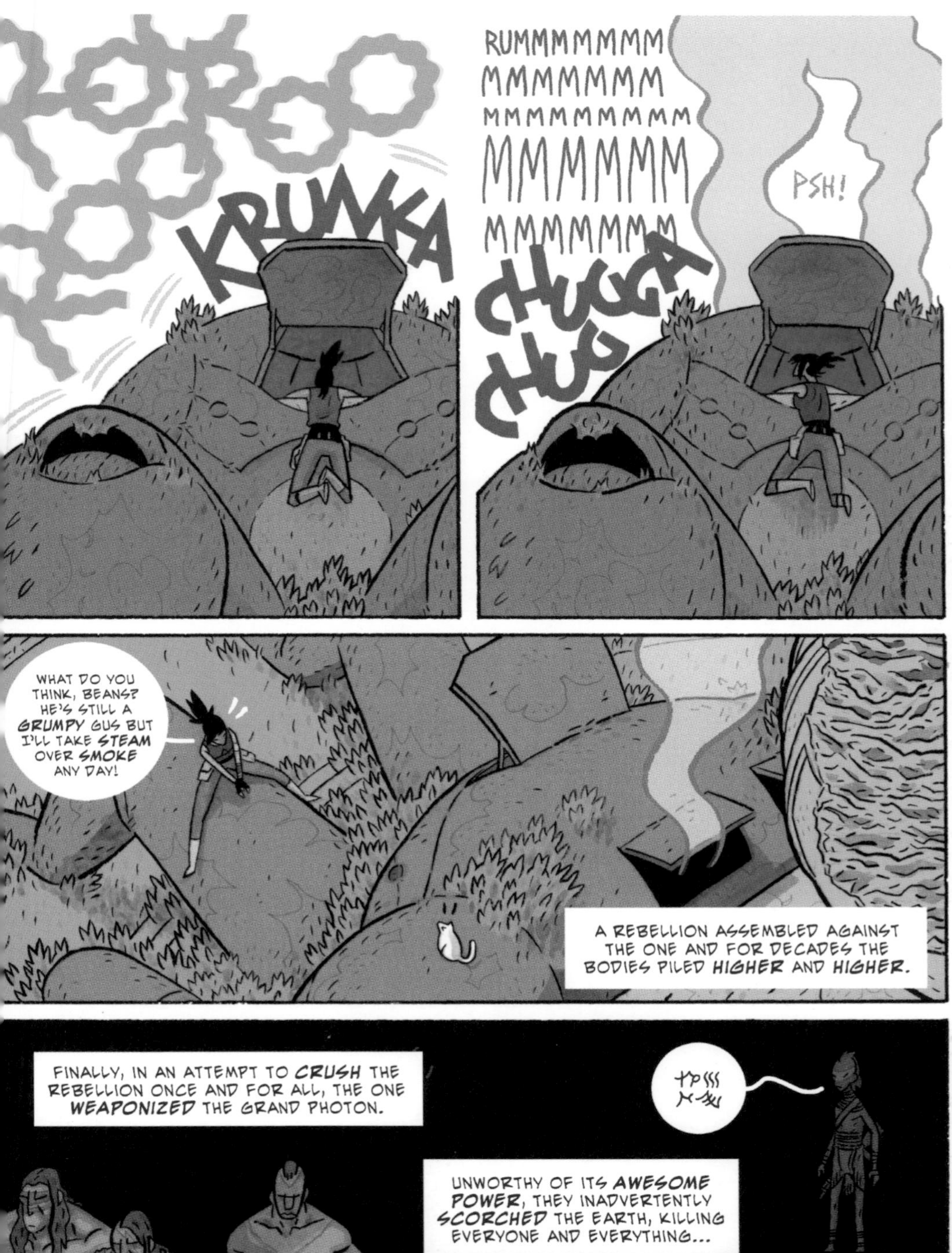
KRUNKA
RUMMMMMMM MMMMMMM MMMMMMMMM MMMMMM MMMMMMM
CHUGGA CHUG
PSH!
WHAT DO YOU THINK, BEANS? HE'S STILL A GRUMPY GUS BUT I'LL TAKE STEAM OVER SMOKE ANY DAY!
A REBELLION ASSEMBLED AGAINST THE ONE AND FOR DECADES THE BODIES PILED HIGHER AND HIGHER.
FINALLY, IN AN ATTEMPT TO CRUSH THE REBELLION ONCE AND FOR ALL, THE ONE WEAPONIZED THE GRAND PHOTON.
UNWORTHY OF ITS AWESOME POWER, THEY INADVERTENTLY SCORCHED THE EARTH, KILLING EVERYONE AND EVERYTHING...
WELL...MOSTLY.

GAH! BAD HOSE!

PROBABLY HAD MICE LIVING IN THE THING.

BEEDLE DOOP DOOP

ANOTHER SIGNAL?!
WELP, LET'S GET OUT IN FRONT OF THIS ONE **BEFORE** IT STARTS LOSING STRENGTH.
boop

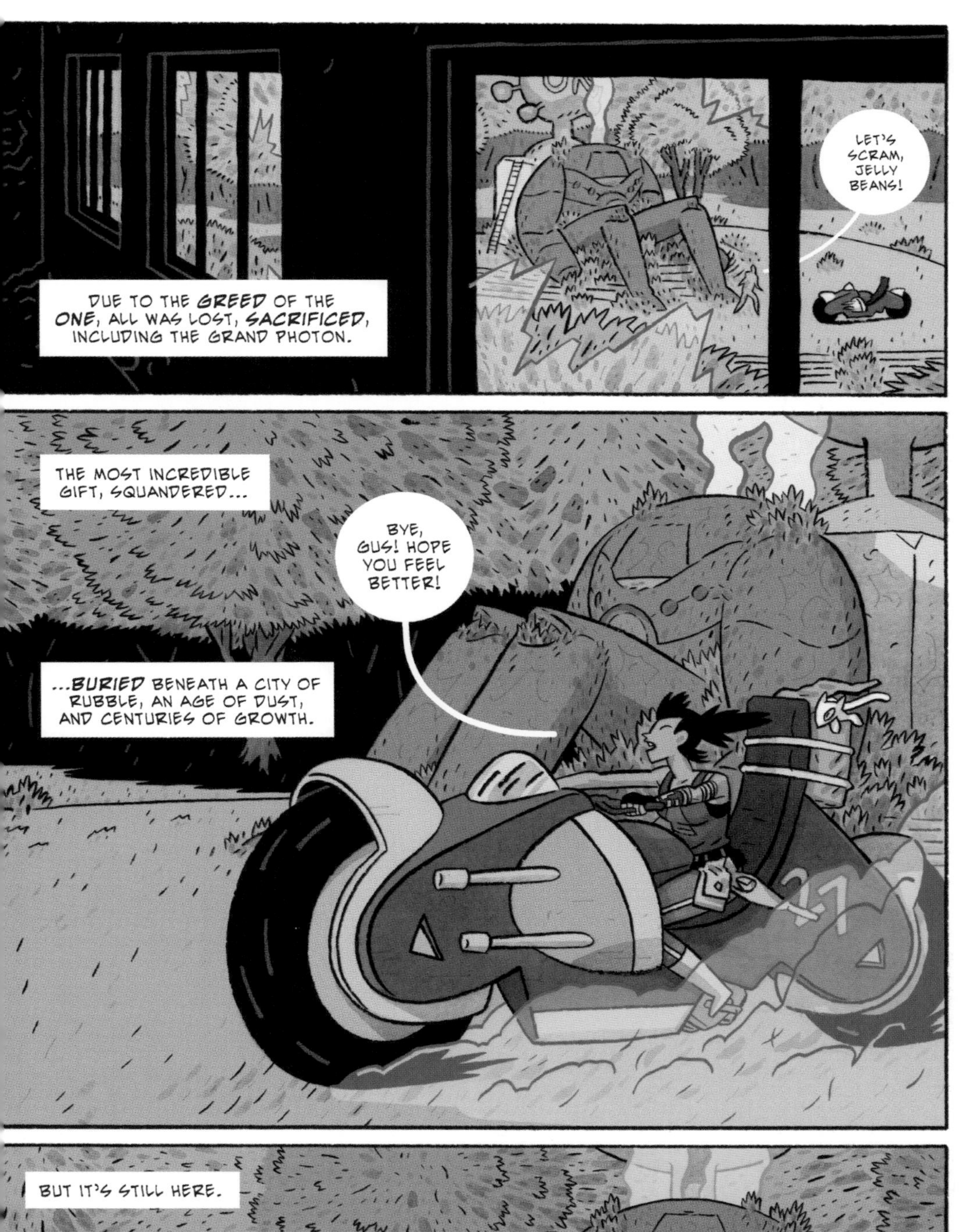
DUE TO THE GREED OF THE ONE, ALL WAS LOST, SACRIFICED, INCLUDING THE GRAND PHOTON.
LET'S SCRAM, JELLY BEANS!
THE MOST INCREDIBLE GIFT, SQUANDERED...
BYE, GUS! HOPE YOU FEEL BETTER!
...BURIED BENEATH A CITY OF RUBBLE, AN AGE OF DUST, AND CENTURIES OF GROWTH.
BUT IT'S STILL HERE.
SOMEWHERE.

I DON'T KNOW WHY I GET SO EXCITED ...
THE TRAIL ALWAYS GOES COLD BEFORE WE CAN GET EVEN **REMOTELY** CLOSE TO THE THING.

H
C

BEANS, BEANS, THE MAGICAL FRUIT--

THE MORE YOU EAT, THE MORE YOU TOOT!
HAHA!
와앙

KEEP UP THE GOOD WORK?

KEEP UP THE GOOD WORK?!

YOU SAID THREE MONTHS!
I'VE BEEN HERE SIX YEARS!

AND ALL YOU OFFER IS--
SMASH
"KEEP UP THE GOOD WORK"?!

WELL, I DON'T CARE ABOUT YOU OR YOUR STUPID "GOOD WORK"!
I DON'T CARE ANY-MORE!

I DON'T CARE!
I JUST WANT TO GO HOME!
J- JELLY ?
BRAKKA BRAKKA BRAKKA BRAKKA BRAKKA BRAKKA BRAKKA BRAKKA BRAKKA BRAKKA

BRAKKA
BRAKKA
PING
PING
CHINK
PING
REEEEEEE

DOODOODOODOODOODOODOODOODOODOODOO
DOODOODOODOODOODOODOODOODOODOODOO

BLORP

ODOODOODOO-KLIKLIKLIKLIKLIK

IT CAME FROM OUT THERE...

BEEDLE DOOP DOOP
YUP.

BRAKKA
BRAKKA
BRAKKA
BRAKKA

!

HHHHH

BRAKKA
BEEDLEDOOPDOOP

LISTEN TO THE TRACKER. FOLLOW THE CHIMES.
OK.
OK.

BEEDLEDOOPDOOP

BEEE DOOP

GAH!
THE TRACKER LOST SIGNAL!

BRAKKAP

OK.
OK.
JUST LISTEN TO HIS FEET.

JUST LISTEN.
LISTEN.
...
JUST LISTEN.

OK. OK.
...
...
OH GOD...

OH GOD. IT'S GONE.

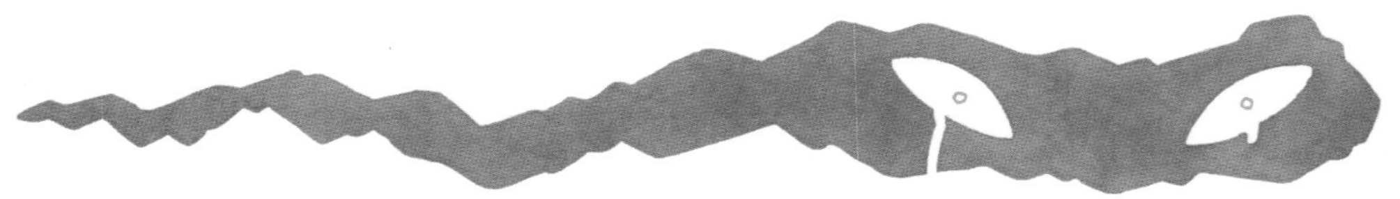

OH, JELLY. WHAT ARE WE GOING TO--

WHA?
JELLY ?!

JELLY, WHERE ARE YOU?!

JELLY BEANS!

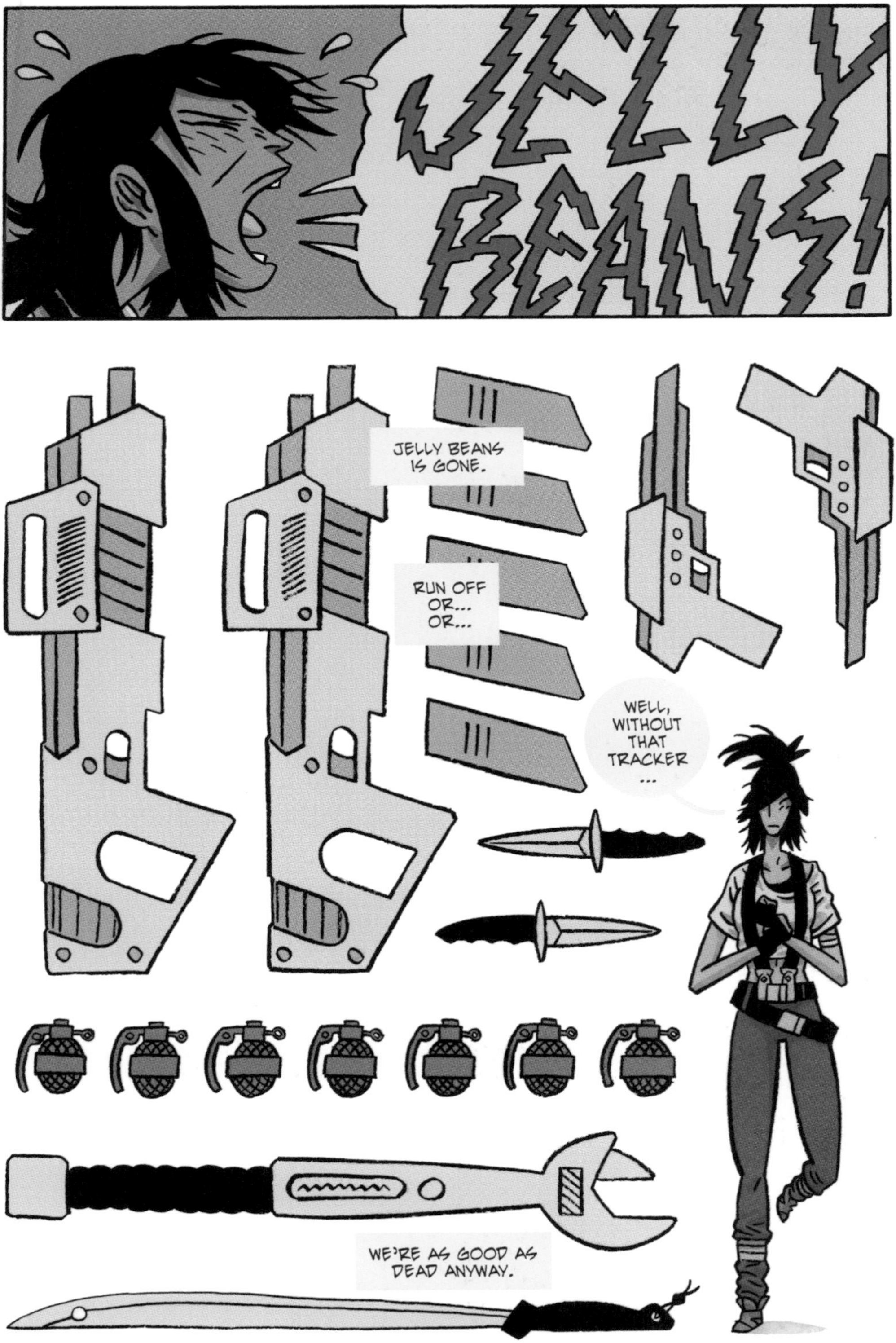

JELLY BEANS IS GONE.
RUN OFF OR... OR...
WELL, WITHOUT THAT TRACKER ...
WE'RE AS GOOD AS DEAD ANYWAY.

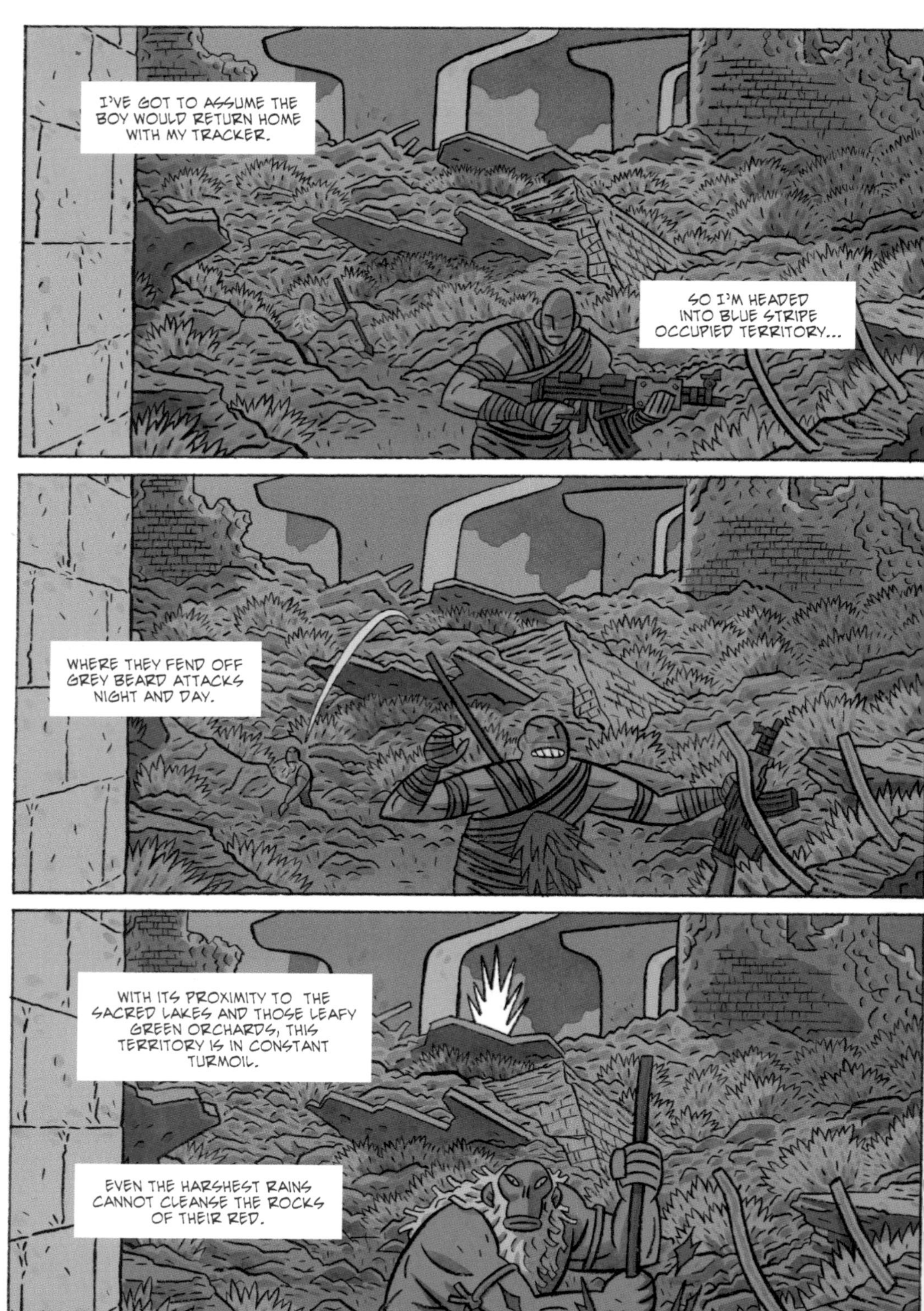
I'VE GOT TO ASSUME THE BOY WOULD RETURN HOME WITH MY TRACKER.
SO I'M HEADED INTO BLUE STRIPE OCCUPIED TERRITORY...
WHERE THEY FEND OFF GREY BEARD ATTACKS NIGHT AND DAY.
WITH ITS PROXIMITY TO THE SACRED LAKES AND THOSE LEAFY GREEN ORCHARDS, THIS TERRITORY IS IN CONSTANT TURMOIL.
EVEN THE HARSHEST RAINS CANNOT CLEANSE THE ROCKS OF THEIR RED.

VVREE EEEEEE

DOO DOO DOO DOO DOO DOO DOO DOO
DOO DOO DOO DOO DOO DOO

BUT I'LL FIND THE BOY...
DOO DOO DOO DOO
KILLING ANYTHING THAT STANDS IN MY WAY.

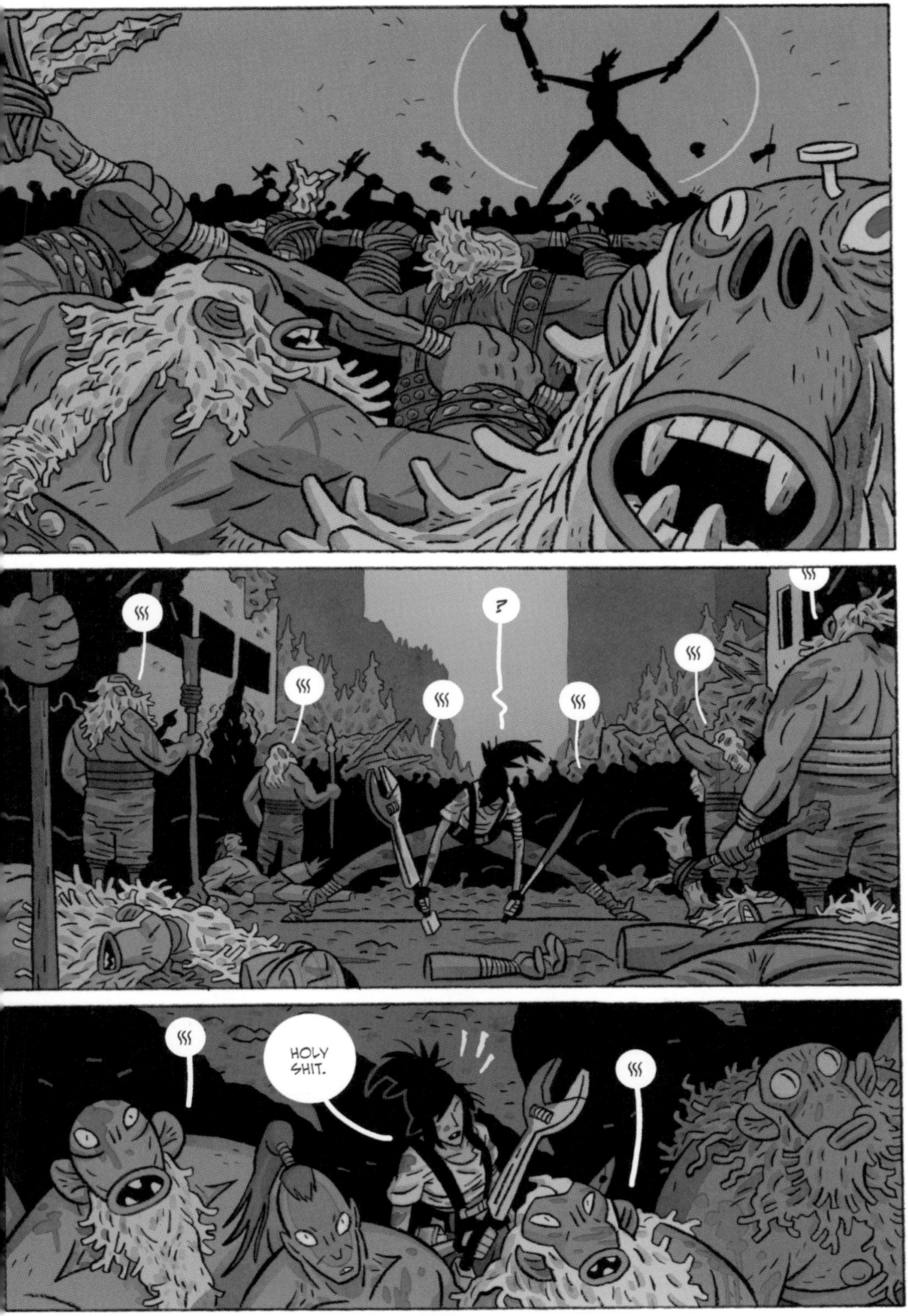

?

HOLY SHIT.

TEARS OF THE SUN.

BOOM

KLOK

ARIA!
BREAKFAST IS READY, HONEY!

...
MOM?

BEEDLE DOOP DOOP

BEEDLE DOOP DOOP

BEEDLE DOOP DOOP

BEEDLE DOOP DOOP

NO.

?.

WHA?
BEEDLE DOOP DOOP

BEEDLE DOOP DOOP

SLICE

RAAAA
AAAAAAAAA
AAAAAAAAA
AAAAAAAAA
AAAAAAAAA
AAAAAHHHH
HHHHHHHH
HHH!!!!!

huff
huff

♪

YOU REALLY WANT TO DO IT THIS WAY?
HE'S WHAT? MAYBE 14 YEARS OLD?
AND YOU KILLED HIS DOGS!
YOU PRACTICALLY BROUGHT THIS ON YOURSELF.
SHUT UP.
SHUT UP.
SHUT UP.

BEEDLE
DOOP
DOOP

I NEED THAT TRACKER !!!
CHOOM

SPLAT

DAMN IT, KID.
DON'T YOU MAKE ME...

...
I'M SORRY.

SPLAT
AH, BUGGER.

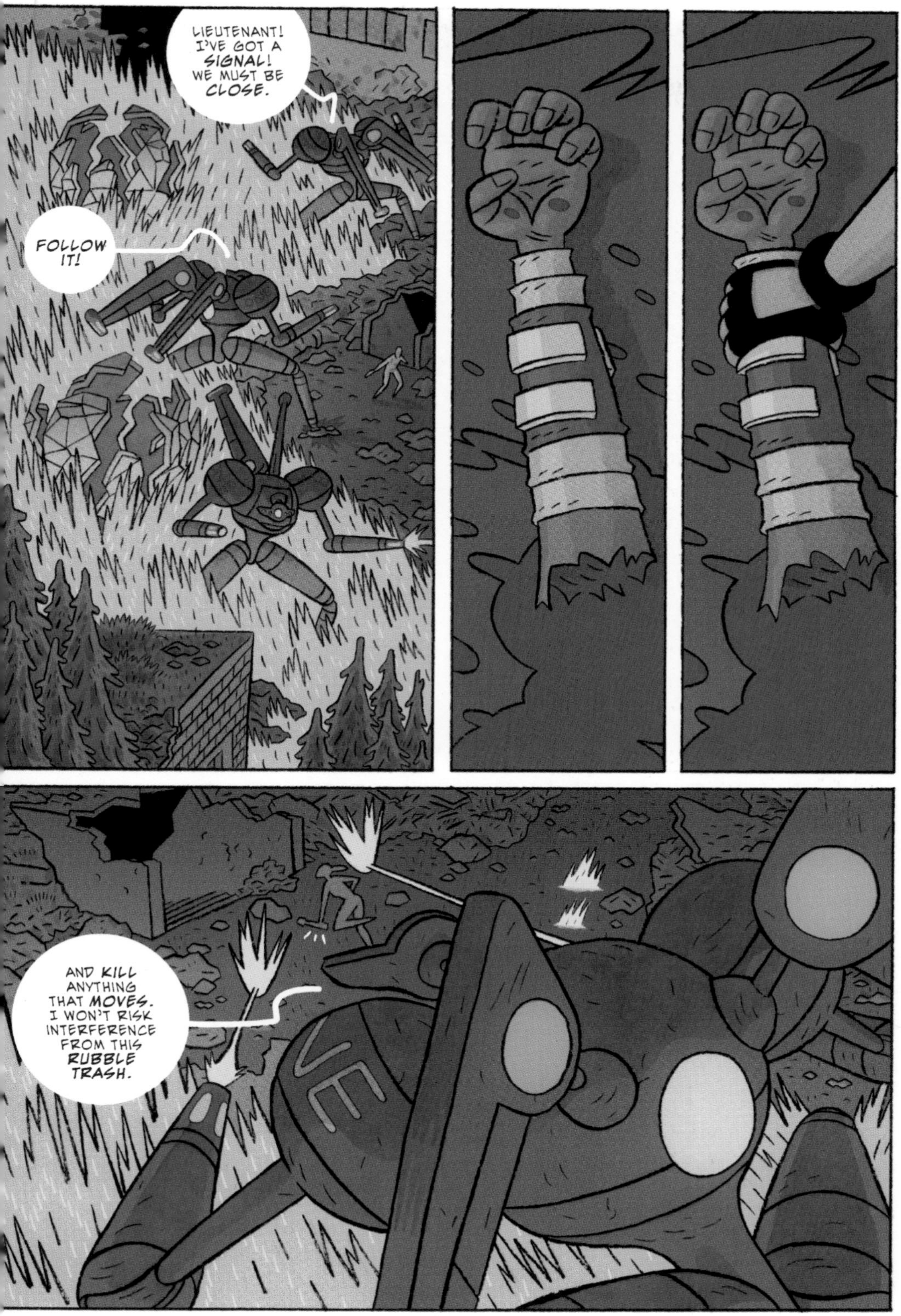

AND KILL ANYTHING THAT MOVES. I WON'T RISK INTERFERENCE FROM THIS RUBBLE TRASH.

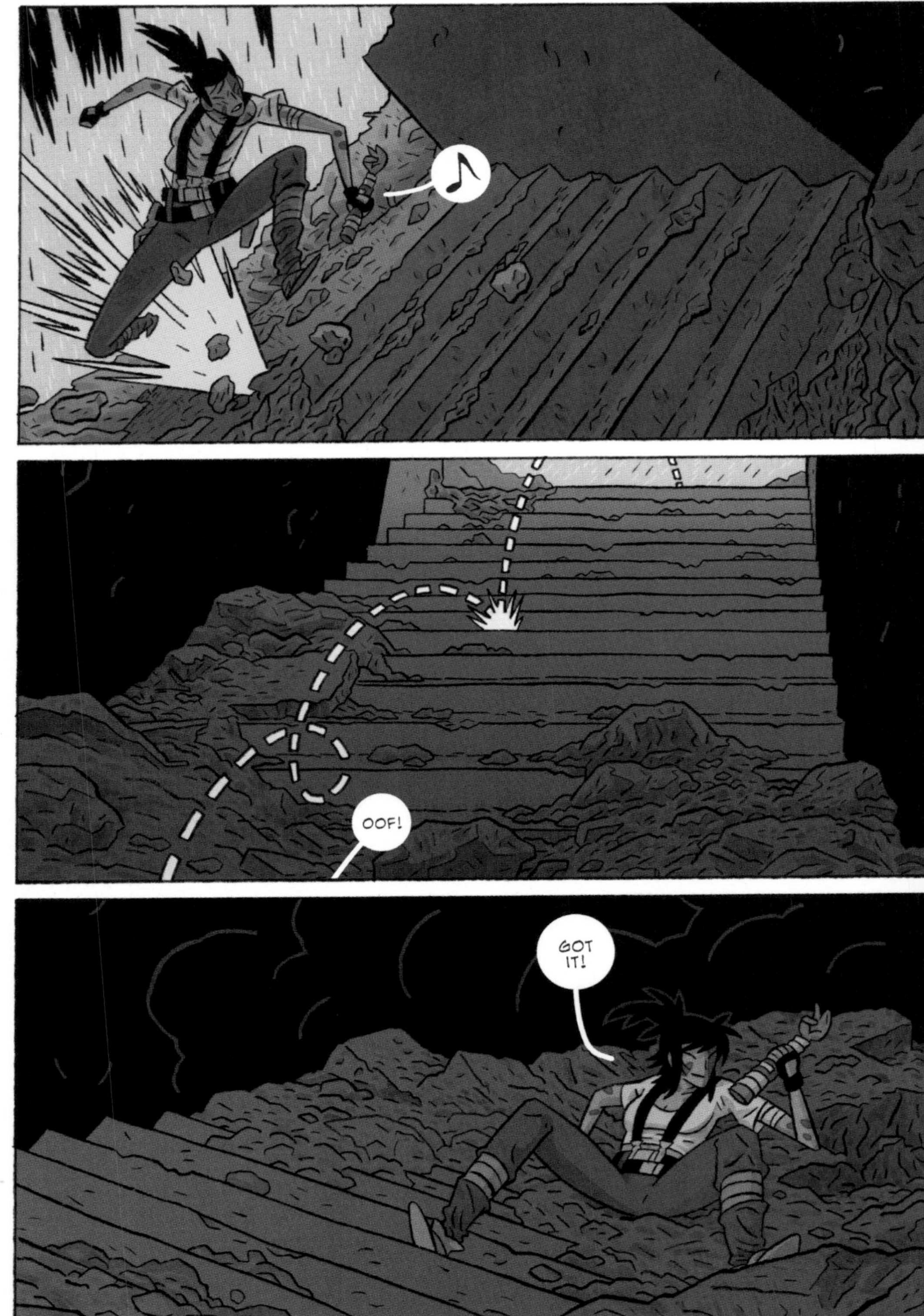
♪
OOF!
GOT IT!

THE ONE.
HMPH! BONEHEADS.

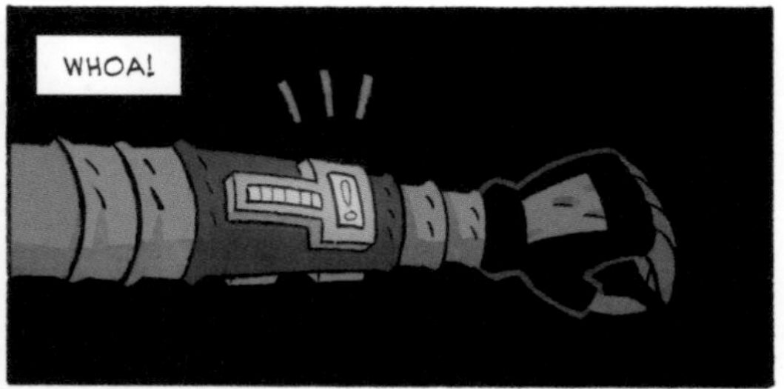

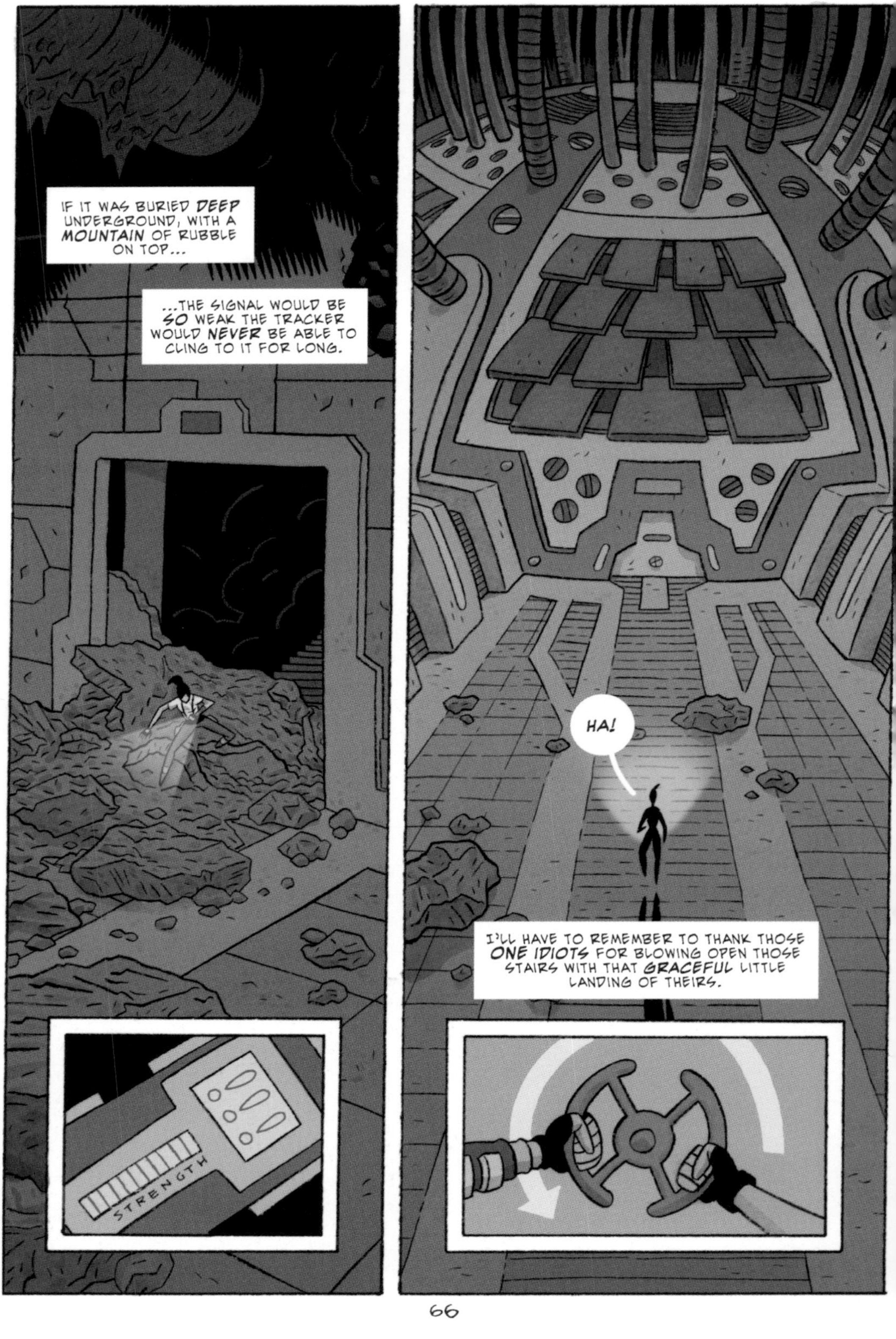

IF IT WAS BURIED **DEEP** UNDERGROUND, WITH A **MOUNTAIN** OF RUBBLE ON TOP...

...THE SIGNAL WOULD BE **SO** WEAK THE TRACKER WOULD **NEVER** BE ABLE TO CLING TO IT FOR LONG.

STRENGTH

HA!

I'LL HAVE TO REMEMBER TO THANK THOSE **ONE IDIOTS** FOR BLOWING OPEN THOSE STAIRS WITH THAT **GRACEFUL** LITTLE LANDING OF THEIRS.

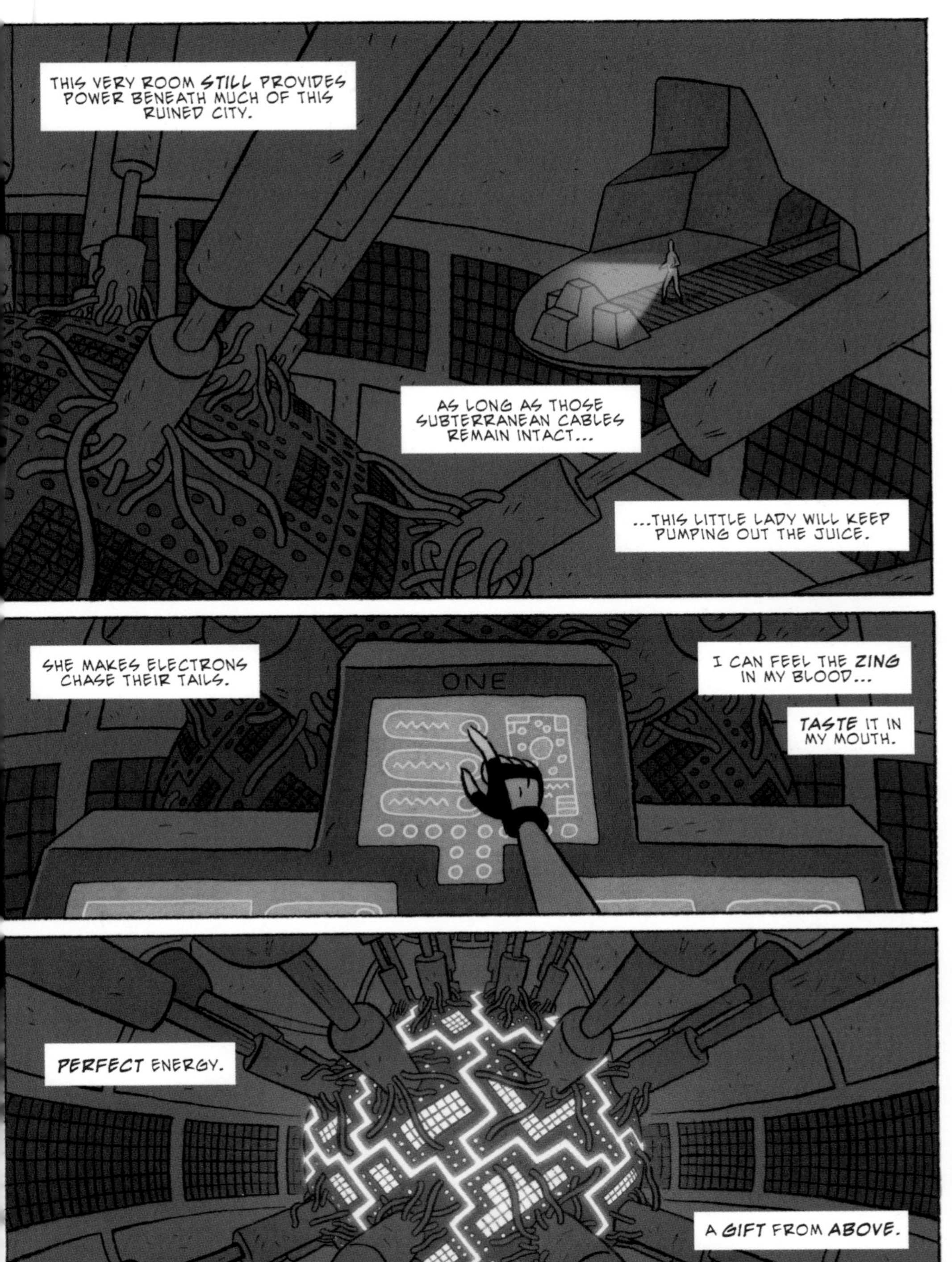
THIS VERY ROOM STILL PROVIDES POWER BENEATH MUCH OF THIS RUINED CITY.
AS LONG AS THOSE SUBTERRANEAN CABLES REMAIN INTACT...
...THIS LITTLE LADY WILL KEEP PUMPING OUT THE JUICE.
SHE MAKES ELECTRONS CHASE THEIR TAILS.
ONE
I CAN FEEL THE ZING IN MY BLOOD...
TASTE IT IN MY MOUTH.
PERFECT ENERGY.
A GIFT FROM ABOVE.

BEHOLD...
THE GRAND PHOTON.
SUSTAINER OF LIFE...
...HARBINGER OF DEATH...
...AND MY TICKET OUT OF HERE.
I'VE GOT TO FIND JELLY BEANS.

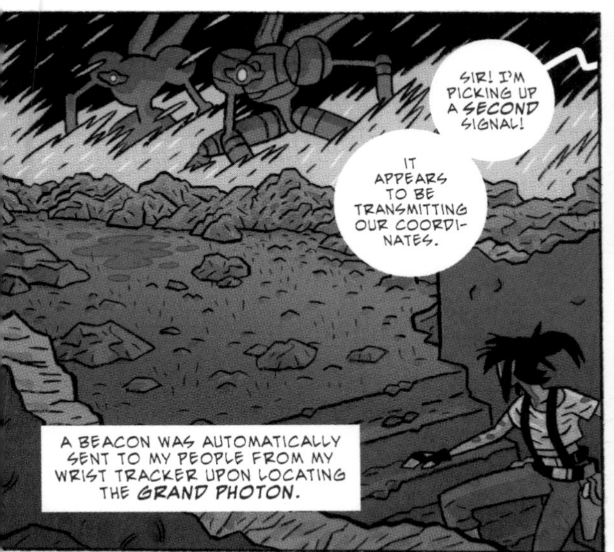
SIR! I'M PICKING UP A SECOND SIGNAL!
IT APPEARS TO BE TRANSMITTING OUR COORDI-NATES.
A BEACON WAS AUTOMATICALLY SENT TO MY PEOPLE FROM MY WRIST TRACKER UPON LOCATING THE GRAND PHOTON.

BING 15 MINUTES REMAIN UNTIL EXTRACTION. CURRENTLY 1,437 FEET SOUTHWEST OF THE EXTRACTION POINT.

BING RETRIEVING CYCLE27.

AFTER SIX YEARS OF WAITING FOR THIS MOMENT, YOU'D THINK I'D HAVE MY BAGS PACKED AND ON THE CURB, READY TO GO.
I HAVE LESS THAN 15 MINUTES TO FIND JELLY AND GET BACK HERE...

...OR MY RIDE LEAVES WITHOUT ME.

THERE! STOP HER!
NOT EXACTLY HOW I PICTURED THIS.

VREEEEEE

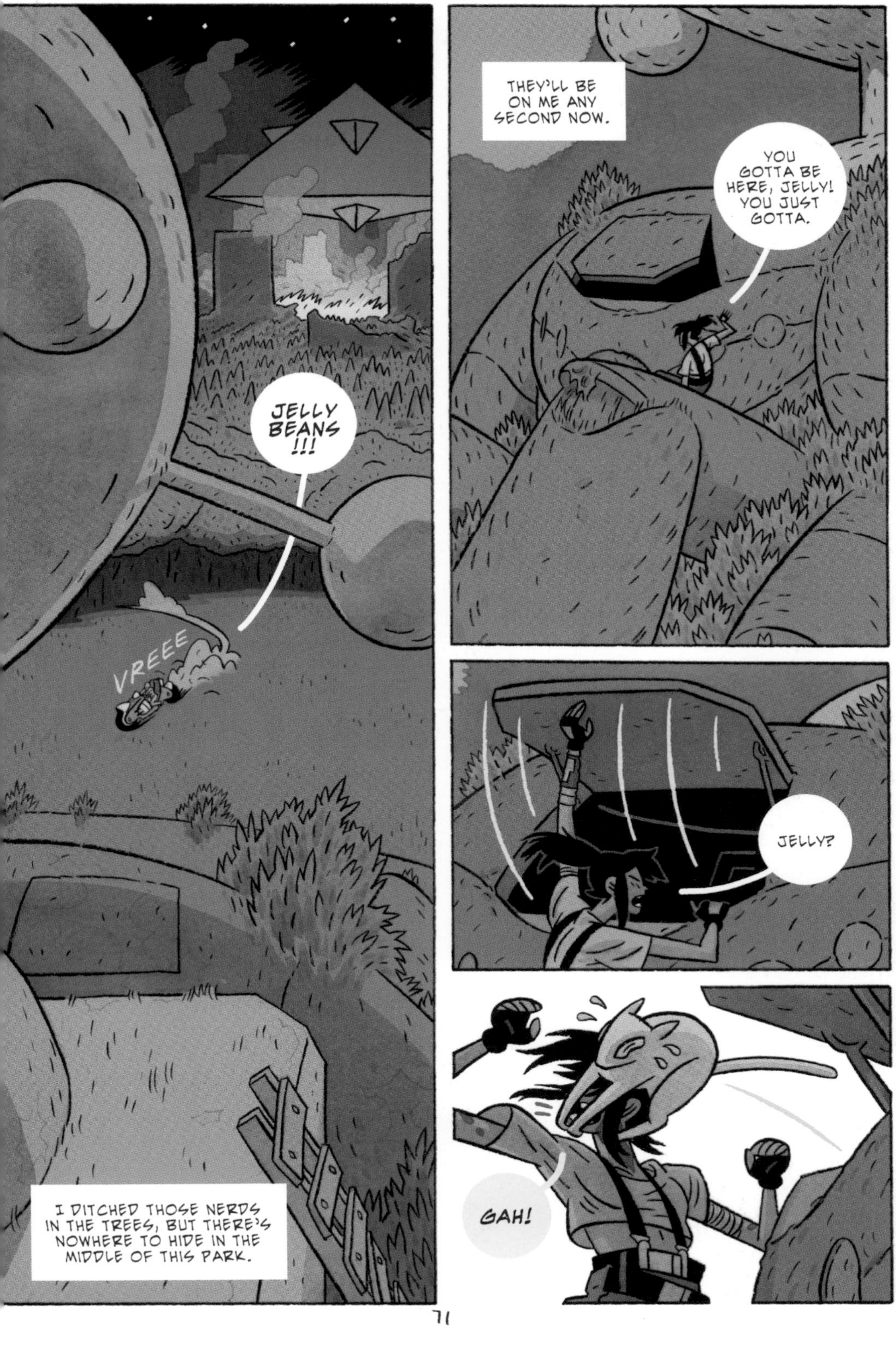

JELLY BEANS !!!

VREEE

I DITCHED THOSE NERDS IN THE TREES, BUT THERE'S NOWHERE TO HIDE IN THE MIDDLE OF THIS PARK.

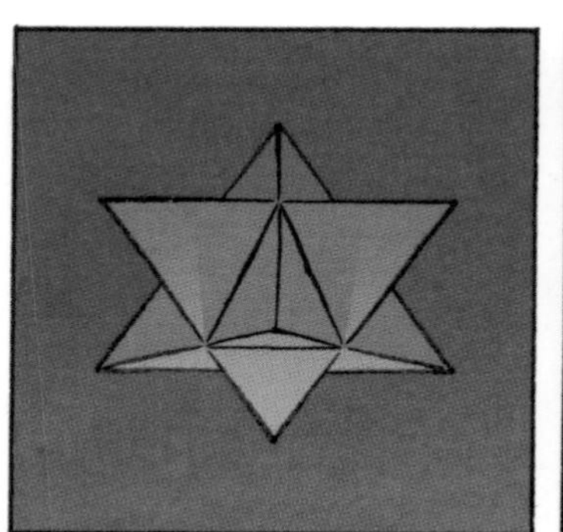

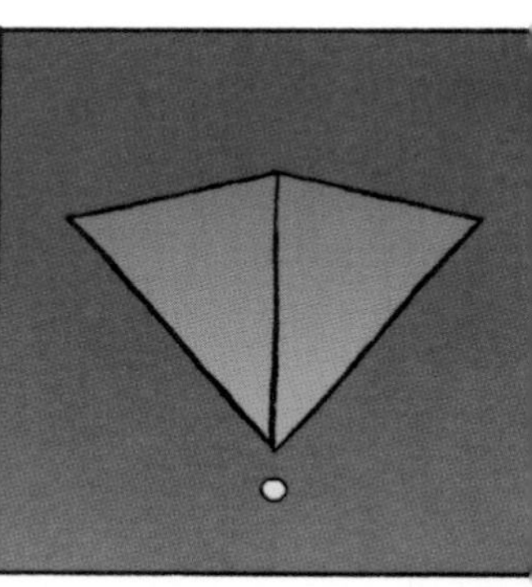

KLINK
CLING
BANG
POP
THUNK
CLING
OK. OK.OK. THINK!
WE'RE SHORT ONE MOUSE-EATEN HOSE. WHAT IF WE...

CHOK

THERE! IN THE MECH!

C'MON. C'MON. C'MON.

WOOT! WOOT!
THAT'S IT, GUS!

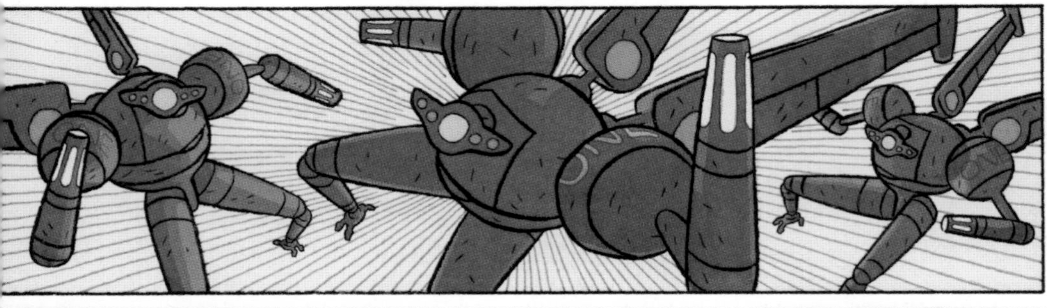

NOW ON YOUR FEET!

GET! UP!

ONE
ONE
ONE
ONE
ONE
ONE
HOLY-SHIT-HERE-WE-GO--

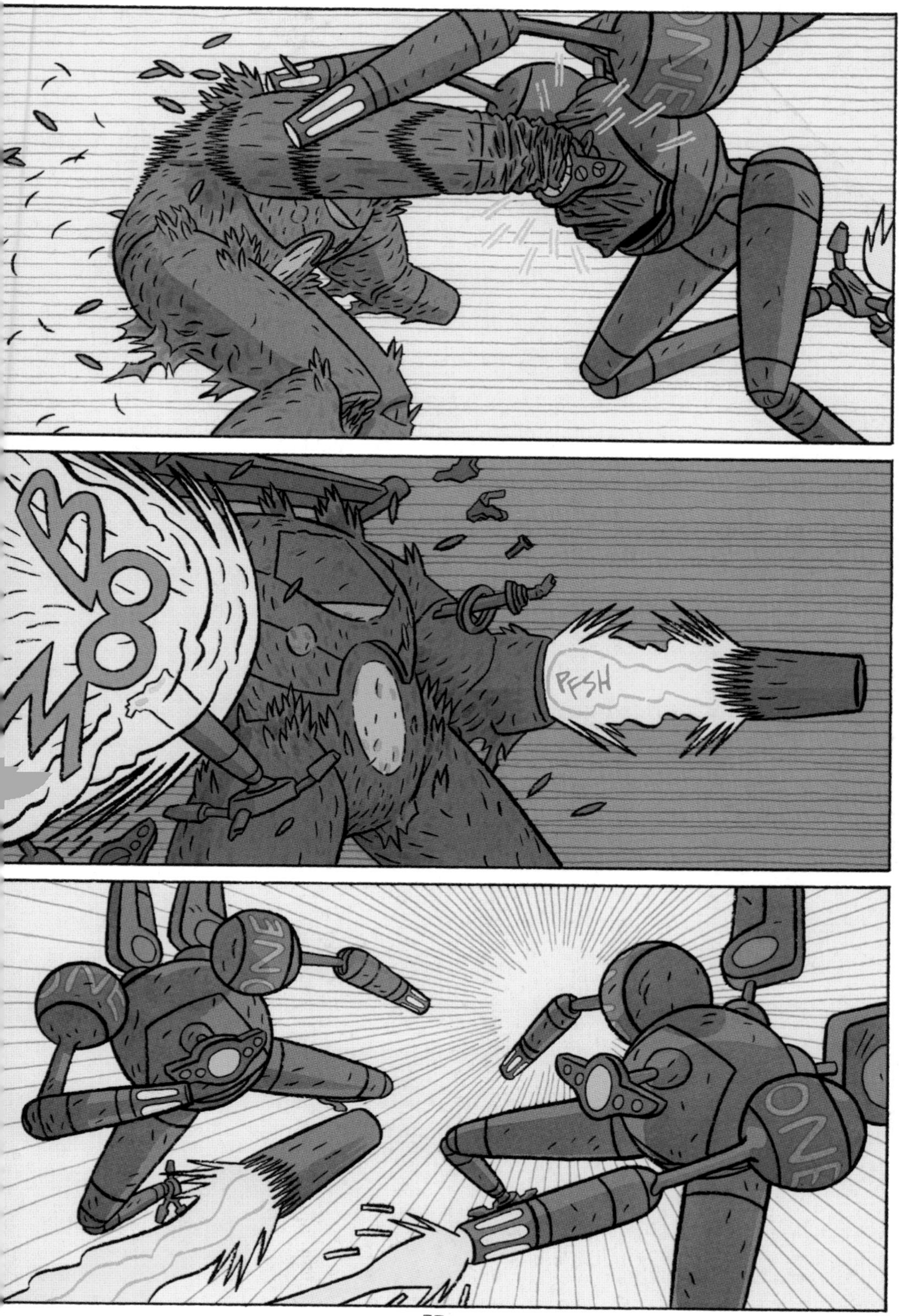

ONE

BOOM
PFSH

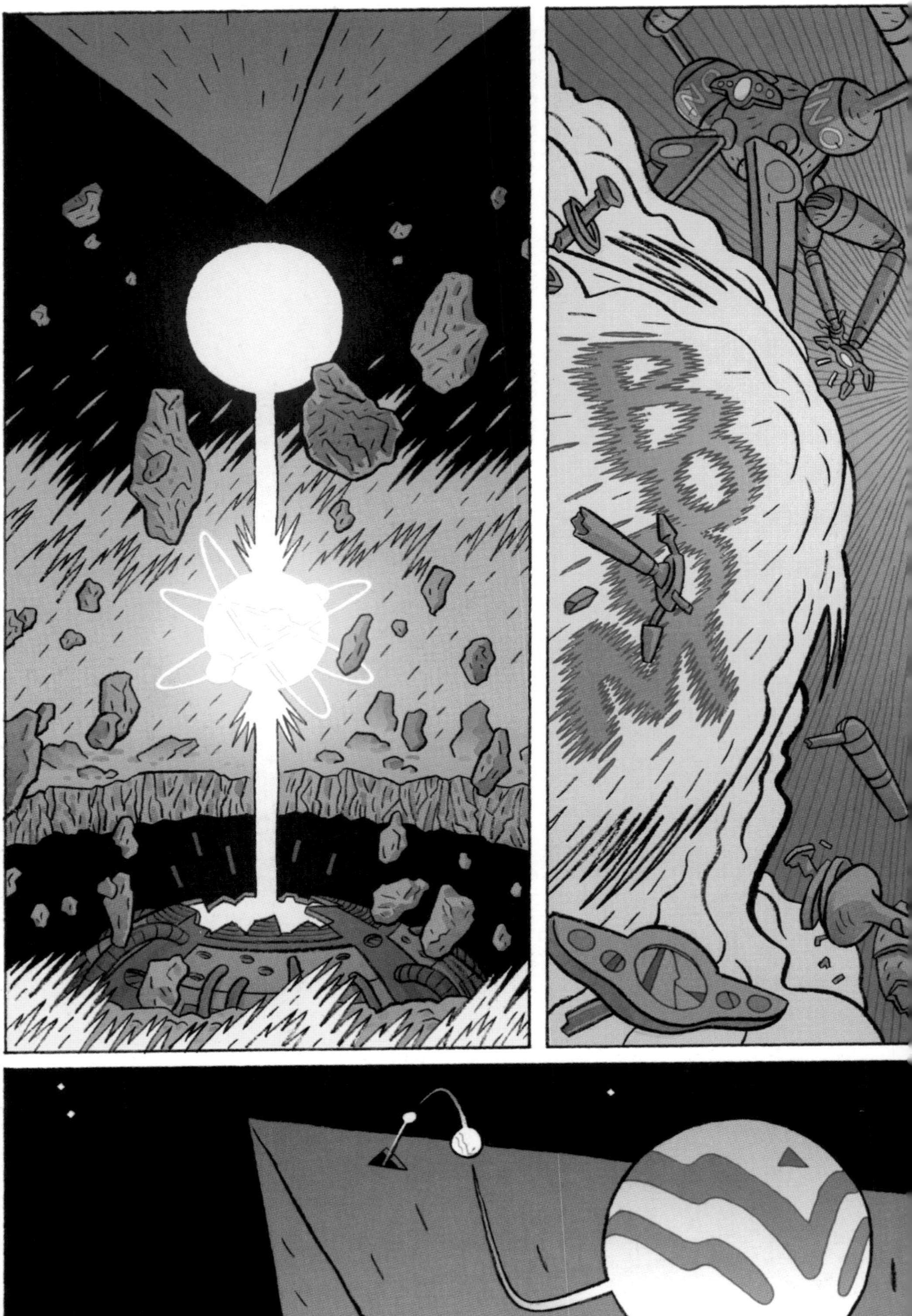

BOOM

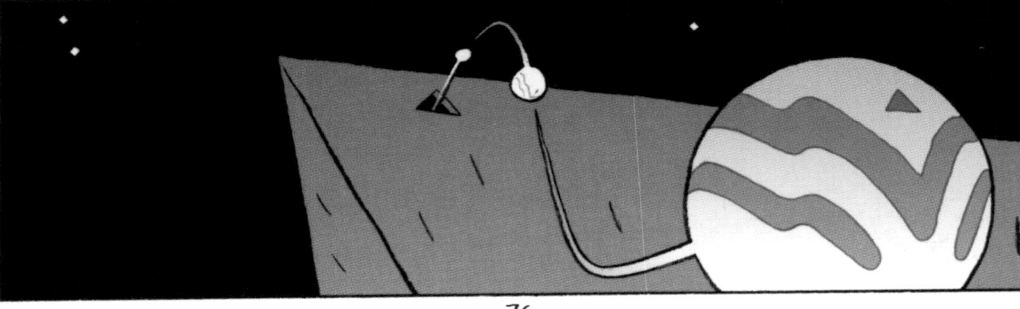

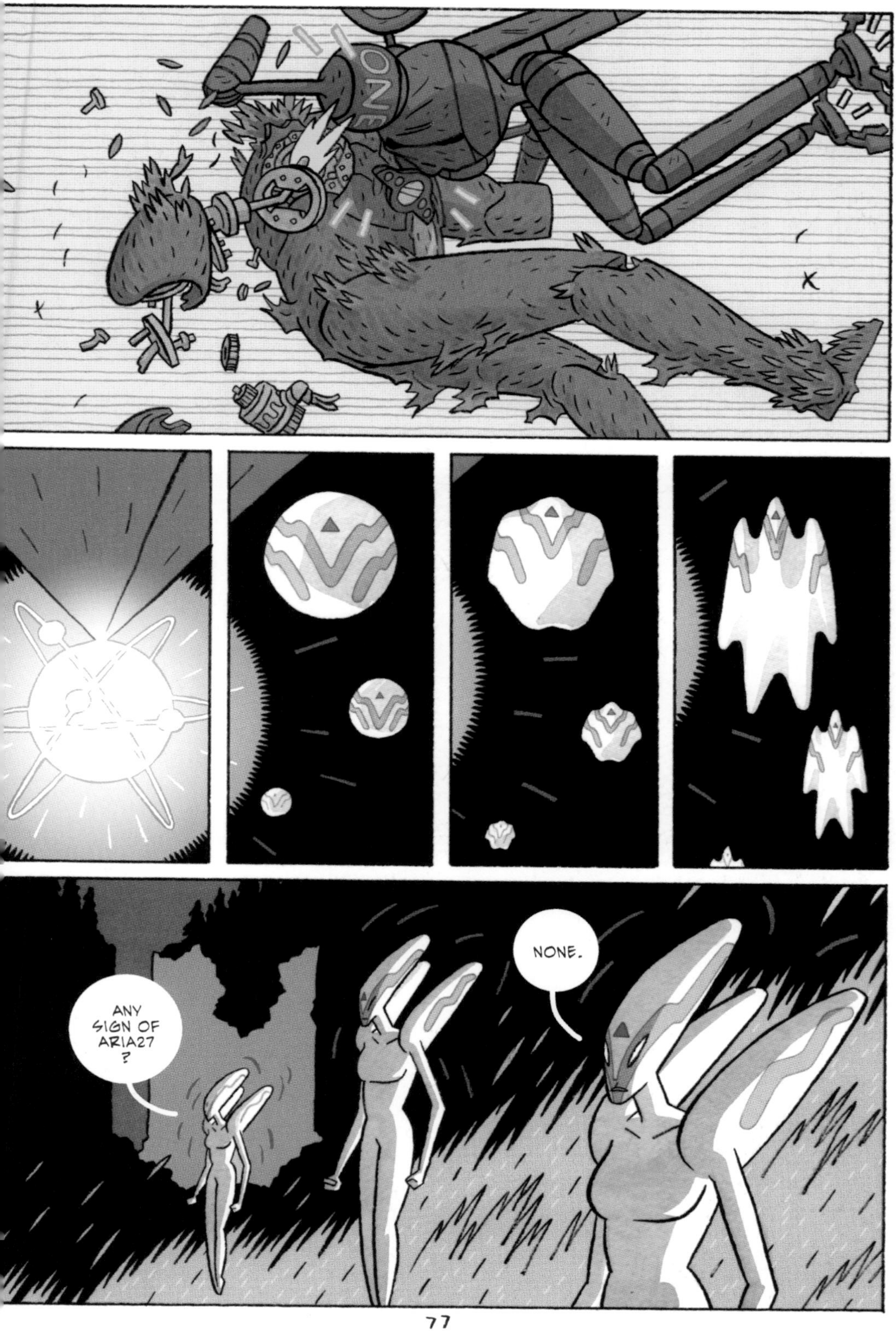

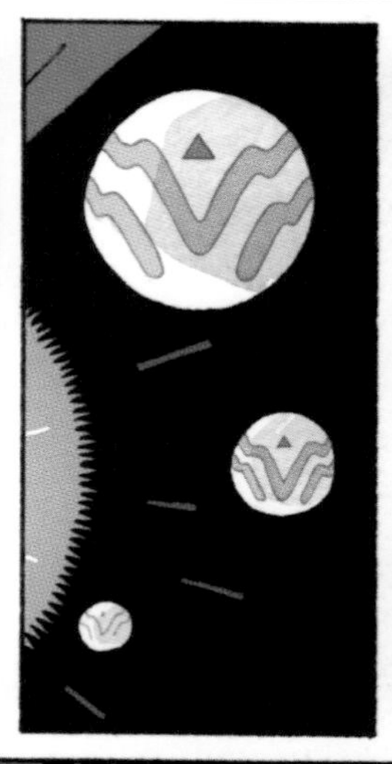

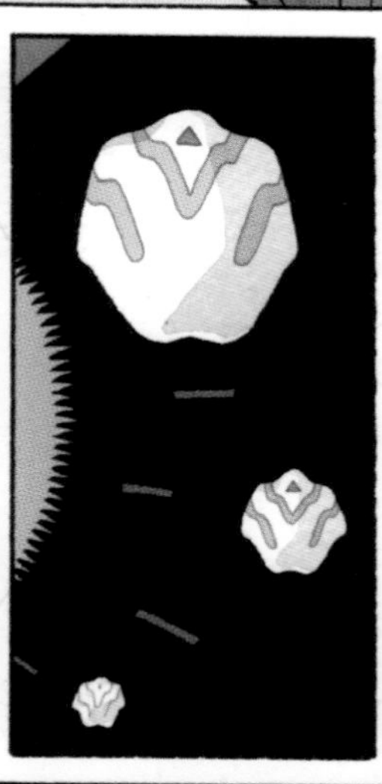

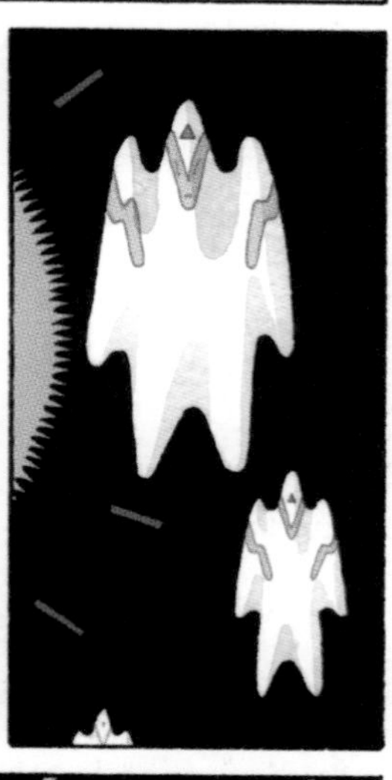

ANY SIGN OF ARIA27 ?
NONE.

SPUT
SPUTTER
SPUT
SPUTTER
SPUT

ARIA27 IS DEAD.
COME. WE MUST MAKE HASTE.
SPUT SPUT
SPUTTER SPUT
WE'VE GOT INCOMING!
SPUTTER
SPUT SPUT
SPUT
SPUTTER

HALT!
COME NO CLOSER.

SPAK
SPAK POP

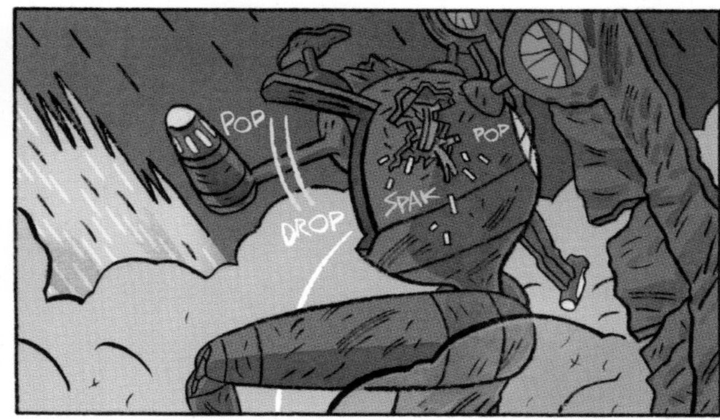
POP
POP
SPAK
DROP

PAK

YOU ARE IN BREACH OF PROTOCOL. WHY DID YOU ABANDON THE EXTRACTION POINT?

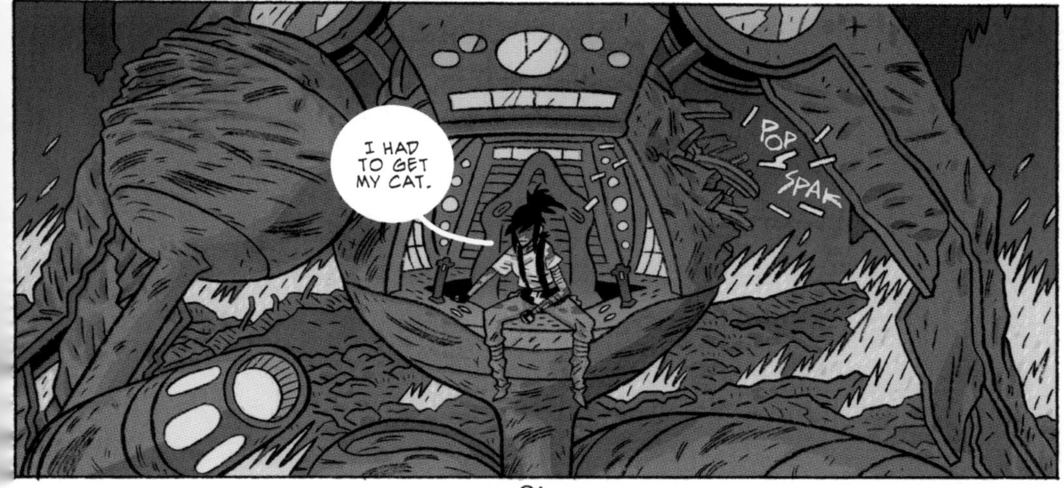
I HAD TO GET MY CAT.
POP
SPAK

E.208

WOW! 412, JELLY! THEY'VE **BUILT** AND **SEEDED** SO MANY OVER THE LAST SIX YEARS!

E.137

096

LICK LICK

E.401

E.411

GREETINGS, ARIA OF 27. EXCELLENT WORK RETRIEVING THE GRAND PHOTON.

CAN THOSE OF EARTH27 RIGHT THEIR CRUMBLING SHIP?

...OR DO WE *DESTROY* 27 BEFORE THEY SPREAD LIKE A *PLAGUE* TO OTHER PLANETS?

E.312

E.312
bing

HA
HA HA HA
HA HA
HA

ONE

skritch
skritch

IF I MAY...

I...I'VE READ YOUR FIELD REPORTS. WHY WOULD YOU SPARE NUMBER 27?

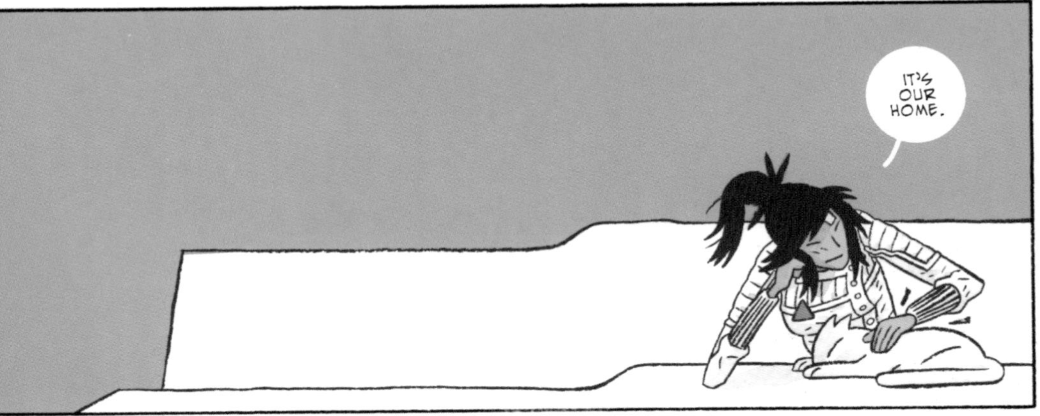

AH! JE RIS DE ME VOIR
SI BELLE EN CE MIROIR,
AH! JE RIS DE ME VOIR
SI BELLE EN CE MIROIR,
EST-CE TOI, MARGUERITE,
EST-CE TOI?
WHAT? STILL SICK OF THAT ONE?
ALL RIGHT, KNUCKLEHEAD. HOW ABOUT ...
...
IN MUSIC, STEMMING FROM THE LATIN ROOT "FIN," MEANING "END," OR ITS COUSIN "FINISH," IT IS NOT UNCOMMON FOR AN ARIA TO END SIMPLY NOTATED WITH THE ITALIAN WORD...
fine
(FEE-NAY)

THANKS:

TO **MIKE RICHARDSON**
AND **DARK HORSE COMICS**,
FOR MAKING THIS WHOLE THING
POSSIBLE AND HELPING ME PUT MY
COMICS INTO READERS' HANDS.

TO MY FRIENDS, THE BRILLIANT CREATORS
JOHN ARCUDI AND **MIKE OEMING**,
FOR TAKING THE TIME TO TALK ABOUT
APOCALYPTIGIRL AND SHARING YOUR
EXTREMELY FLATTERING THOUGHTS.

TO MY FRIEND AND EDITOR, **JIM**,
FOR HELPING ME TAKE *ARIA* FROM ITS
INFANCY TO WHAT YOU NOW HOLD.

AND TO MY BEST FRIEND
AND WIFE, **ERIN**, FOR YOUR ENDLESS
SELFLESSNESS. VERY FEW WOULD KNOW,
UNDERSTAND, OR EMULATE THE SACRIFICES
YOU MADE (AND CONTINUE TO MAKE)
THROUGHOUT THE PROCESS OF PUTTING
THIS TOGETHER. I HOPE I CAN SOMEDAY
REPAY YOU IN SOME SMALL WAY.